A Conservative Primer on Government and Economics

(with Notes from Frederick Bastiat's Political Economy Essays)

Catherine McGrew Jaime

Books by Catherine Jaime include:

A Brief Financial History of the United States

Understanding the U.S. Constitution

Understanding the Electoral College

Failure in Philadelphia?

Copyright 2013 by Catherine McGrew Jaime

www.CatherineJaime.com

Creative Learning Connection

8006 Old Madison Pike, Ste 11-A

Madison, AL 35758

www.CreativeLearningConnection.com

Table of Contents

Introduction	2
A Good Law?	4
Proper Role of Government	5
Cost of Government	6
How Big Is Too Big?	7
Foundations of Government	9
Separation of Church and State	11
Pursuit of Happiness	13
What is Compassion?	14
Individual Responsibility	16
Winners & Losers	18
Prices	20
Care Vs. Insurance	22
Mountains of Debt	24
What's a Fair Share?	25
Government as Robin Hood	27
Class Warfare	29
Incentives	31
Property Rights	33
Unintended Consequences	35
Outsourcing	37
Greed/Self Interest	39
Profit	41
Conclusion	43
Notes from Bastiat's Essays	44
About the Author	85

Introduction

I spend much time every week helping highschoolers to gain a better understanding of the workings of the U.S. government, and the reality of economic principles. As I do, I often marvel at their level of understanding versus the lack of understanding I often run into elsewhere – both among teens and adults.

~^~^~

This little booklet (the first section was originally published as "There Ought to Be a Law") is a simple look at topics that are too important to be constantly lost in boring textbooks and complicated lectures. Clearly this is not meant to be an exhaustive look, but rather a brief introduction.

It comes from the very basic belief that the U.S. Constitution was, and continues to be, the foundation of our government. Without such a firm foundation, our government is on very shaky ground.

~^~^~

The first section is followed by excerpts from Frederick Bastiat's *Essays on Political Economy*. Bastiat was an early nineteenth century French economist; you will quickly note that the more things change, the more they stay the same.

A Good Law?[1]

A good idea does not equal a good law.

Yes, we want people to wear seat belts, exercise, and eat certain types of foods over other foods. But how do any of those fall under the very short list of things that government should be regulating?

Hint: They don't!

~^~^~

"As government expands, liberty contracts."

Ronald Reagan,
U.S. President

---

[1] For Bastiat's commentary on "Why Laws" – see page 57.

Proper Role of Government[2]

One of the primary goals of government should be the protection of individual rights, not the trampling of those rights. We should look at each act of government through this lens: is it protecting or trampling individual rights?

~^~^~

"Government exists to protect us from each other. Where government has gone beyond its limits is in deciding to protect us from ourselves."

Ronald Reagan,
U.S. President

---

[2] For Bastiat's commentary on "What is Government?" – see page 46.

Cost of Government

One of the first things we should ask when anyone talks about the government doing anything (at the local, state, or federal level): "How much will it cost and who is going to pay for it?"

~^~^~

"A government big enough to give you everything you want is a government big enough to take from you everything you have."

Gerald R. Ford,
U.S. President

How Big Is Too Big?

With government, big is not better. I believe, as our founders believed, that we need government to provide for our common defense and promote the general welfare (but not to guarantee it), and not much more.

In Article One of the Constitution, the framers went to great lengths to spell out the limits of the law- making portion of the federal government. They had little fear of giving the government too little power, but great concern of giving it too much.

"We the people of the United States, in order to form a more perfect union, establish justice, insure domestic tranquility, provide for the common defense, promote the general welfare, and secure the blessings of liberty to ourselves and our posterity, do ordain and establish this Constitution for the United States of America."

**Preamble
to the Constitution**

Foundations of Government

From our founding the Declaration of Independence and the Constitution have been, and should continue to be, the bedrock of our government, **not** the U.N., and not foreign laws or foreign ideas.

Corollary: The Constitution in general and the Bill of Rights in particular, were written to protect citizens from the government, not the other way around.

"Government is a trust, and the officers of the government are trustees. And both the trust and the trustees are created for the benefit of the people."
Henry Clay (1777 – 1852)
U.S Rep & Senator from Kentucky

Separation of Church and State

A "wall of separation" between the church and the state is not in the constitution. The phrase was originally written by Thomas Jefferson in a letter to the Danbury Baptist Church in response to a letter they had written him. In Jefferson's letter, when he refers to the wall of separation, he was promising to protect the church from government, not government from the influence of religion.

So the current talk of "separation of church and state" is not only not what the first amendment says, it isn't what Jefferson said.

"We hold these truths to be self-evident, that all men are created equal, that **they are endowed by their Creator** with certain unalienable Rights, that among these are Life, Liberty and the pursuit of Happiness."
    Declaration of Independence

Pursuit of Happiness

The Declaration of Independence talks about the right to "life, liberty, and the **pursuit** of happiness" – not "life, liberty, **and** happiness."

Contrary to what many people act like, government's role is **not** to give us happiness. And it will not succeed at something for which it has no constitutional mandate.

"I predict future happiness for Americans, if they can prevent the government from wasting the labors of the people under the pretense of taking care of them."
Thomas Jefferson,
U.S. President

What is Compassion?

True compassion is giving people a hand up, not a handout. But even if we believed that handouts were really equal to compassion, where would the government get the authority to do give them?

We need to go back to the very important, and very basic, concept that the powers not specifically given to the federal government are reserved for the states and the people (see the 10th Amendment to the U.S. Constitution if that seems odd to you.) To see the types of powers that are granted to the Federal Government, check out Article One, Section Eight of the Constitution. You may be surprised at how short the list is!

~^~^~

"I am for doing good to the poor, but...I think the best way of doing good to the poor, is not making them easy in poverty, but leading or driving them out of it. I observed...that the more public provisions were made for the poor, the less they provided for themselves, and of course became poorer. And, on the contrary, the less was done for them, the more they did for themselves, and became richer."

Benjamin Franklin,
Printer, Author, Founding Father

Individual Responsibility

Just as we want the government to insure individual rights, we don't want it to interfere with individual responsibility. Our belief in individual responsibility goes deep – back to our Greco-Roman and Judeo-Christian roots.

We don't need (or want) government to tell us who to marry, or what job to take, nor do we need it to tell us how much school we need or how much food to eat. We need to be left alone to take responsibility for our own actions – including the risks and successes resulting from the choices we make.

~^~^~

"And we can celebrate when we have a government that has earned back the trust of the people it serves...when we have a government that honors our Constitution and stands up for the values that have made America, America: economic freedom, individual liberty, and personal responsibility."[3]

John Boehner,
Congressman

---

[3] For Bastiat's commentary on "Liberty" – see page 69.

Winners & Losers[4]

Our government does not, and should not, exist to pick winners and losers. But that's what happens when "bailouts" and "stimulus plans" enter the government's budget.

Corollary: "No one is too big to fail." When the government bails out a company, for instance, the auto industry bailouts, the company can continue to make the same fiscally irresponsible decisions that got it in trouble in the first place.

~^~^~

---

[4] For Bastiat's commentary on "Using the Law" – see page 64.

"Those who manage their way into a crisis are not necessarily the right people to manage their way out of a crisis."

Albert Einstein,
Scientist

~^~^~

"The government is merely a servant -- merely a temporary servant; it cannot be its prerogative to determine what is right and what is wrong, and decide who is a patriot and who isn't. Its function is to obey orders, not originate them."

Mark Twain,
Author

Prices[5]

In a free market, price is king! Or at least it is when the government doesn't interfere. But when the government places price ceilings (exa: gasoline prices after a hurricane), the predictable result is shortages. Conversely, when the government sets price floors, surplus is the necessary result. A prime example of that is when the government sets a minimum price at which labor can be sold (minimum wage), thereby setting a price floor. The predictable result is a surplus of labor.

~^~^~

---

[5] For Bastiat's commentary on "Liberty of Exchange" – see page 74.

"The first lesson of economics is scarcity. There is never enough of anything to satisfy all those who want it. The first lesson of politics is to disregard the first lesson of economics."

Thomas Sowell,
Economist

Care Vs. Insurance

Health Care is not the same thing as Health Insurance, though for several years the two terms have been used interchangeably. Everyone may need/desire access to good health care, but that does not equal the need for universal health insurance. Making health care truly affordable requires bringing the price down. But the price will only go down if the supply is increased. (Or if the government mandates lower prices – but like with other price ceilings that will cause a shortage instead!)

"My reading of history convinces me that most bad government results from too much government."
Thomas Jefferson,
U.S. President

Mountains of Debt

When the federal government borrows money to pay for programs it cannot currently afford, it is stealing from future generations. A balanced budget would be one of the greatest gifts we could give to our children and grandchildren.

~^~^~

"I, however, place economy among the first and most important republican virtues, and public debt as the greatest of the dangers to be feared."
Thomas Jefferson,
U.S. President

What's a Fair Share?[6]

"Rich" people already pay more taxes (and a higher percentage) than poor people. For those crying for them to pay their "fair share," I ask: at what point will they be considered to be paying their fair share? 60% 70% 80%? Even if we continue to raise the rates on the rich, there are not enough of "them" to fund all the government programs that people can imagine. What we're really accomplishing here is a simple "redistribution of wealth," and we should call it what it is.

---

[6] See Bastiat's commentary on this in the middle of "Plunder and the Government" – on page 54.

"The problem with socialism is that you eventually run out of other people's money."
Margaret Thatcher,
British Prime Minister

Government as Robin Hood[7]

Something "free" from the government is never really. Anything given away as "entitlement" has to first be taken from someone else.

If an individual took our money against our will, we would call it stealing, but when the government takes it by force, we call it taxes. But what's the real difference? (Yes, some taxes are necessary to run the government, but when it is actually the redistribution of wealth, there is nothing in the Constitution to support it.)

---

[7] For Bastiat's commentary on "Plunder" – see page 51.

"Government's view of the economy could be summed up in a few short phrases: If it moves, tax it. If it keeps moving, regulate it. And if it stops moving, subsidize it."

Ronald Reagan,
U.S. President

Class Warfare

Class warfare has no place in the United States. We should not be talking about lower class and middle class as if we have some sort of caste society where people are stuck in one place or another. The terms "lower income" and "upper income" are much more meaningful.

In the U.S. people can move from one income level to another, and many will do exactly that over the course of their lifetimes. While it may not be the case in many other societies, here when we make less money than someone else, it should not cause envy, but rather rejoicing that we may someday have the opportunity to attain a higher income level as well.

~^~^~

"An economy hampered by restrictive tax rates will never produce enough revenue to balance our budget, just as it will never produce enough jobs or enough profits."

John F. Kennedy,
U.S. President

~^~^~

"The wise and correct course to follow in taxation and all other economic legislation is not to destroy those who have already secured success but to create conditions under which everyone will have a better chance to be successful."

Calvin Coolidge,
U.S. President

Incentives

People react to incentives and disincentives. If we incentivize them to do something, we shouldn't act surprised when they do it!

Corollary: If incentives change, choices will change.

Example: When prices go up, we are incentivized to conserve, just as when prices go down, we are incentivized to use more of something.

"Incentive – nothing less than the interest one has in his own improvement – will mold the future just as surely as it shaped the past."
Lawrence W. Reed,
Economist

Property Rights[8]

One of the most important concepts in economically-sound societies is the idea of property rights. If we don't own it, can we ever really build on it, improve it, or create with it? Where is our incentive if we don't have the rights to our own property?

In the early seventeenth century the Pilgrims tried a very brief and quite unsuccessful attempt at limiting property rights. Famine and hunger increased, rather than decreased, in this perfect example of "the tragedy of the commons." The solution was simple and effective: families were given their own plots of land, and the responsibilities

---

[8] For Bastiat's commentary on "Property Rights" – see page 62.

and rights that went with them.

~^~^~

"Ultimately property rights and personal rights are the same thing."
Calvin Coolidge,
President

~^~^~

"Among the natural rights of the colonists are these: First a right to life, secondly to liberty, and thirdly to property: together with the right to defend them in the best manner they can."
Samuel Adams,
Patriot, Founding Father

Unintended Consequences[9]

The long term effects of government policies seem seldom to be considered. We would also do well to consider what the "unintended consequences" may be.

For example, an unintended consequence of the "Cash for Clunkers" plan was to decrease the supply of used vehicles available for sale, raising prices on that scarce item, and hurting the very people the program claimed to aid – those in lower income brackets.

~^~^~

---

[9] For Bastiat's commentary on "Seen" vs. "Not Seen" – see page 50.

"The art of economics consists in looking not merely at the immediate but at the longer effects of any act or policy; it consists in tracing the consequences of that policy not merely for one group but for all groups."

Henry Hazlitt,
Economist

Outsourcing

How many people oppose outsourcing because it sends jobs overseas, but approve the idea of foreign aid? Outsourcing is the best form of foreign aid – helping a country through the power of the market.

And while it sounds good to say that as a country we should be independent, will that ever be the case? Or should we strive for interdependence?

"We can erect walls to foreign trade and even discourage job-displacing innovation. Time and again through our history, we have discovered that attempting merely to preserve the comfortable features of the present--rather than reaching for new levels of prosperity--is a sure path to stagnation."

Alan Greenspan,
Chairman of the Federal Reserve

Greed/Self Interest

Much is made of greed and self-interest, as if they are a bad thing. But do we really expect humans to act in any other way? Which of the following quotes do you believe?

~^~^~

"We have always known that heedless self-interest was bad morals; we now know that it is bad economics."
Franklin D. Roosevelt,
U.S. President

~^~^~

"It is not from the benevolence of the butcher, the brewer, or the baker, that we expect our dinner, but from their regard to their own self-interest."

Adam Smith,
Economist

Profit

Along those lines, is making a profit a bad thing? If not, why is it so often demonized? If so, do we really expect companies to stay in business without making a profit?

Just as Adam Smith's baker and butcher have their own self-interest in mind while they conduct business, so do bigger companies. That is not evil, it is logical.

Only the market, through profits and losses, can efficiently lead a company to pursue innovation. When losses or insufficient profits occur, a company is motivated to pursue alternative methods or machines, find cheaper inventory, or discover other money saving options.

~^~^~

"In a truly great company profits and cash flow become like blood and water to a healthy body: They are absolutely essential for life but they are not the very point of life."
Jim Collins,
Author

Conclusion to this First Portion

I hope this has helped you think more deeply about your own ideas of economics and government.

I was influenced by studying many of our founders, including George Washington, the first president of the United States, who put it so well when he said: *"A primary object should be the education of our youth in the science of government. In a republic, what species of knowledge can be equally important? And what duty more pressing than communicating it to those who are to be the future guardians of the liberties of the country?"*

I hope you now enjoy the excerpts from and comments on Frederick Bastiat's, "Political Economy Essays," which make up the second half.

Notes from Frederick Bastiat's *Essays on Political Economy*

Edited by

Catherine McGrew Jaime

Introduction to Notes

I had read much of Bastiat's essay, The Law, *many years ago, and remembered it as being well written, but I was still surprised when I recently stumbled upon his* Essays on Political Economy *(written shortly before his death in 1850). I was looking for a few nuggets, a few good quotes or ideas, to help finish up an economics book I was working on.*

Instead I felt like I had stumbled into a political and economic gold mine. It was difficult to believe these words were written in France over 160 years ago. I was frustrated that I had never read them before, never had the opportunity to share them with my students, or discuss them with friends.

As I worked through page after page of his thoughts, I was impressed and I was motivated to share them with others. I have selected highlights from his essay to share with interested readers. I hope you enjoy his insight on government and politics, interrupted only occasionally by my own limited commentary.

Please Note: My comments are in italics and I have bolded a number of Bastiat's extremely significant points along the way.

What is Government? What is the Proper Use of Government?

Bastiat pulled no punches when he described government and what it can and cannot accomplish: "**I should be glad enough, you may be sure, if you had really discovered a beneficent and inexhaustible being, calling itself the Government, which has bread for all mouths,**

work for all hands, capital for all enterprises, credit for all projects, oil for all wounds, balm for all sufferings, advice for all perplexities, solutions for all doubts, truths for all intellects, diversions for all who want them, milk for infancy, and wine for old age--**which can provide for all our wants,** satisfy all our curiosity, **correct all our errors, repair all our faults,** and exempt us henceforth from the necessity for foresight, prudence, judgment, sagacity, experience, order, economy, temperance and activity...

...Indeed, the more I reflect upon it, the more do I see that nothing could be more convenient than that we should all of us have within our reach an inexhaustible source of wealth and enlightenment--**a universal physician, an unlimited treasure, and an infallible counselor, such as you describe**

Government to be...

...For **no one would think of asserting that this precious discovery has yet been made,** since up to this time everything presenting itself under the name of the Government is immediately overturned by the people, precisely because it does not fulfill the rather contradictory conditions of the program." *Can it be better put than the way Bastiat put it? And 160 years later Government is no more successful than it was then!*

He continued, "...But let us go to the root of the matter. We are deceived by money. To demand the co-operation of all the citizens in a common work, in the form of money, is in reality to demand a concurrence in kind; for every one procures, by his own labour, the sum to which he is taxed.

Now, if all the citizens were to be

called together, and made to execute, in conjunction, a work useful to all, this would be easily understood, their reward would be found in the result of the work itself. But, after having called them together, if you force them to make roads which no one will pass through, palaces which no one will inhabit, and this under the prefect of finding them work, it would be absurd, and they would have a right to argue, 'with this labour we have nothing to do; we prefer working on our own account.'"

Public vs. Private

Bastiat continued: "Society is the total of the **forced or voluntary** services which men perform for each other; that is to say, of **public services and private services.**" *We are often taught that public services* *are somehow better than private ones, and yet if we remember that public services actually only come by force, we may be in a better position to evaluate the difference.*

Bastiat explained more about these public enterprises: "Then you will understand that a public enterprise is a coin with two sides. Upon one is engraved a laborer at work, with this device, that which is **seen**; on the other is a laborer out of work, with the device, that which is **not seen**."

*Bastiat understood, even if we don't, that labor done by a "public servant," is not being done by a private one! He spoke often in his writings of the importance of not just what is **seen**, but also what is **not seen**. Too many political decisions are made primarily based on what is **seen** – but what is **not seen** because it happens below the surface, in the longer term,* *or is actually something that doesn't happen as a result – those are often even more important than the short term, visible results of a new policy or law.*

The Introduction of Plunder

As he continued, Bastiat was moving closer to the idea of government plunder. "...Man recoils from trouble--from suffering; and yet he is condemned by nature to the suffering of privation, if he does not take the trouble to work. He has to choose, then, between these two evils. What means can he adopt to avoid both? There remains now, and there will remain, only one way, which is, **to enjoy the labor of others...**
This is the origin of slavery and of plunder, whatever its form may be--whether that of wars,

impositions, violence, restrictions, frauds, etc.--monstrous abuses, but consistent with the thought which has given them birth. Oppression should be detested and resisted--it can hardly be called absurd."

Plunder and the Government

He goes on to show that when socialists get control of Government, plunder becomes legalized: "...The oppressor no longer acts directly and with his own powers upon his victim. No, our conscience has become too sensitive for that. The tyrant and his victim are still present, but there is an intermediate person between them, which is the Government--that is, the Law itself.

What can be better calculated to silence our scruples, and, which is perhaps better appreciated, to overcome all resistance? We all, therefore, put in our claim, under some pretext or other, and apply to Government. **We say to it, 'I am dissatisfied at the proportion between my labor and my enjoyments. I should like, for the sake of restoring the desired equilibrium, to take a part of the possessions of others. But this would be dangerous. Could not you facilitate the thing for me?**

Could you not find me a good place? or check the industry of my competitors? or, perhaps, lend me gratuitously some capital, which you may take from its possessor? Could you not bring up my children at the public expense? or grant me some prizes? or secure me a competence when I have attained my fiftieth year? **By this means I shall gain my end with an easy conscience, for the law will have acted for me, and I shall**

have all the advantages of plunder, without its risk or its disgrace!'"

But is plunder by the government really so different than that by outlaws? Other than that it is harder to fight against!

Bastiat goes on to show so clearly that wealth redistribution through high taxes is merely legalized plunder: "...**Government is the great fiction, through which everybody endeavors to live at the expense of everybody else**...Government is not slow to perceive the advantages it may derive from the part which is entrusted to it by the public. It is glad to be the judge and the master of the destinies of all; it will take much, for then a large share will remain for itself; it will multiply the number of its agents; it will enlarge the circle of its privileges; it will end by appropriating a ruinous proportion.

"**But the most remarkable part**

of it is the astonishing blindness of the public through it all. When successful soldiers used to reduce the vanquished to slavery, they were barbarous, but they were not absurd. Their object, like ours, was to live at other people's expense, and they did not fail to do so. **What are we to think of a people who never seem to suspect that…plunder…is no less criminal because it is executed legally and with order; that it adds nothing to the public good; that it diminishes it, just in proportion to the cost of the expensive medium which we call the Government?**

…It is radically impossible for it to confer a particular benefit upon any one of the individualities which constitute the community, without inflicting a greater injury upon the community as a whole….

Thus, the public has two hopes, and Government makes two

promises--many benefits and no taxes. Hopes and promises, which, being contradictory, can never be realized....

These two promises are forever clashing with each other; it cannot be otherwise. To live upon credit, which is the same as exhausting the future, is certainly a present means of reconciling them: **an attempt is made to do a little good now, at the expense of a great deal of harm in future.** But such proceedings call forth the specter of bankruptcy, which puts an end to credit.

What is to be done then? Why, then, the new Government takes a bold step; it unites all its forces in order to maintain itself; it smothers opinion, has recourse to arbitrary measures, ridicules its former maxims, declares that it is impossible to conduct the administration except at the risk of being unpopular; in short, it proclaims itself governmental." *How prophetic were Bastiat's words.... Is this not exactly what we see today?*

Why Laws?

Most of us take laws, and the need for laws, for granted. But Bastiat explains them in a new way: **"It is not because men have made laws, that personality, liberty, and property exist. On the contrary, it is because personality, liberty, and property exist beforehand, that men make laws.**

Nature, or rather God, has bestowed upon every one of us the right to defend his person, his liberty, and his property, since these are the three constituent or preserving elements of life; elements, each of which is rendered complete by the others, and cannot be understood without them.

"...Now, labor being in itself a pain, and man being naturally inclined to avoid pain, it follows, and history proves it, that **wherever plunder is less burdensome than labor, it prevails; and neither religion nor morality can, in this case, prevent it from prevailing. When does plunder cease, then? When it becomes less burdensome and more dangerous than labour.**

It is very evident that the proper aim of law is to oppose the powerful obstacle of collective force to this fatal tendency; that all its measures should be in favor of property, and against plunder....It would be impossible, therefore, to introduce into society a greater change and a greater evil than this-- the conversion of the law into an instrument of plunder."

As Bastiat has explained so well, Governments should exist to protect us from plunder, not to legalize plunder!

"...**No society can exist unless the laws are respected to a certain degree, but the safest way to make them respected is to make them respectable.**

When law and morality are in contradiction to each other, the citizen finds himself in the cruel alternative of either losing his moral sense, or of losing his respect for the law--two evils of equal magnitude, between which it would be difficult to choose.

"...**Look at the United States. There is no country in the world where the law is kept more within its proper domain--which is, to secure to everyone his liberty and his property."**

If this could be said of us in 1850, can it still be said of us in 2013?
"Therefore, there is no country in the world where social order appears to

rest upon a more solid basis.

Nevertheless, **even in the United States, there are two questions, and only two, which from the beginning have endangered political order.** And what are these two questions? **That of slavery and that of tariffs**; that is, precisely the only two questions in which, contrary to the general spirit of this republic, law has taken the character of a plunderer.

Slavery is a violation, sanctioned by law, of the rights of the person..." *So, prior to the Civil War, Bastiat saw our biggest problems in the U.S. as slavery and tariffs. Slavery is no longer legal, but what has replaced it? With taxes ever on the rise, aren't we becoming slaves to the government now instead?*

Legal Plunder is Still Plunder

"...It is absolutely necessary that this question of legal plunder should be determined, and there are only three solutions of it: 1.When the few plunder the many. 2.When everybody plunders everybody else. 3.When nobody plunders anybody. **Partial plunder, universal plunder, absence of plunder, amongst these we have to make our choice.**" *Again, the simplicity with which he narrows down our choices – no plunder, partial plunder or universal plunder – there really are no other options!*

"**The law can only produce one of these results.**

Partial plunder.--This is the system which prevailed so long as the elective privilege was partial--a system which is resorted to to avoid the invasion of socialism.

Universal plunder.--We have

been threatened by this system when the elective privilege has become universal; the masses having conceived the idea of making law, on the principle of legislators who had preceded them.

Absence of plunder.--This is the principle of justice, peace, order, stability, conciliation, and of good sense, which I shall proclaim with all the force of my lungs (which is very inadequate, alas!) till the day of my death." *Might we see the day that enough others today can make the same claim.*

Plunder vs. Property Rights

"Before I proceed, I think I ought to explain myself upon the word plunder. I do not take it, as it often is taken, in a vague, undefined, relative, or metaphorical sense. I use it in its scientific acceptation, and as expressing the opposite idea to property. **When a portion of wealth passes out of the hands of him who has acquired it, without his consent, and without compensation, to him who has not created it, whether by force or by artifice, I say that property is violated, that plunder is perpetrated."** *And I could not agree with him more.*

"...**When law and force keep a man within the bounds of justice, they impose nothing upon him but a mere negation. They only oblige him to abstain from doing harm.** They violate neither his personality his liberty, nor his property. They only guard the personality, the liberty, the property of others. They hold themselves on the defensive; they defend the equal right of all...

...A friend of mine once

remarked to me, to say that the aim of the law is to cause justice to reign, is to use an expression which is not rigorously exact. **It ought to be said, the aim of the law is to prevent injustice from reigning**....

It is not justice which has an existence of its own, it is injustice. The one results from the absence of the other." *So, Government should exist to protect us from injustice, but is that the way most people see it today?*

Using the Law

"...You say, 'There are men who have no money,' and you apply to the law. **But the law is not a self-supplied fountain, whence every stream may obtain supplies independently of society. Nothing can enter the public treasury, in favor of one citizen or one class,**

but what other citizens and other classes have been forced to send to it."

I have complained for some time now that Government has no money of its own to spend; it can only spend what it takes from others. Wouldn't the understanding of that principle change our perspective on what Government should and shouldn't do? "

If everyone draws from it only the equivalent of what he has contributed to it, your law, it is true, is no plunderer, but it does nothing for men who want money--it does not promote equality. **It can only be an instrument of equalization as far as it takes from one party to give to another, and then it is an instrument of plunder.**

Examine, in this light, the protection of tariffs, prizes for encouragement, right to profit, right to labour, right to assistance, right to instruction, progressive taxation, gratuitousness of credit, social workshops, and you will always find at the bottom legal plunder, organized injustice.

You say, 'There are men who want knowledge,' and you apply to the law. But **the law is not a torch which sheds light abroad which is peculiar to itself.** It extends over a society where there are men who have knowledge, and others who have not; citizens who want to learn, and others who are disposed to teach.

It can only do one of two things: either allow a free operation to this kind of transaction, i.e., let this kind of want satisfy itself freely; or else force the will of the people in the matter, and take from some of them sufficient to pay professors commissioned to instruct others gratuitously. But, in this second case, there cannot fail to be a violation of liberty and property,--legal plunder." *So, where in this, is the argument for things that now seem to be taken for granted, like "public education"?*

Government vs. Private

"...Socialism, like the old policy from which it emanates, confounds Government and society. **And so, every time we object to a thing being done by Government, it concludes that we object to its being done at all.** We disapprove of education by the State--then we are against education altogether. We object to a State religion--then we would have no religion at all. We object to an equality which is brought about by the State--then we are against equality, etc., etc.

They might as well accuse us of

wishing men not to eat, because we object to the cultivation of corn by the State." *When I first read this we had just been involved in this argument in one of my classes. Someone had proposed abolishing the Department of Education. Those who were aghast at the idea accused those who favored it of being against education! But that was not their position – they were merely against education being provided by the state (along with food, housing, medical care, and today the list goes on.)*

"How is it that the strange idea of making the law produce what it does not contain--prosperity, in a positive sense, wealth, science, religion--should ever have gained ground in the political world?" *There seems to be an even greater push now for Government to grant these things to its citizens.*

"If it is true that a great prince is

a rare thing, how much more so must a great lawgiver be?" *I have been reading Machiavelli's* The Prince *recently and believe it would be safe to say that Machiavelli and Bastiat viewed princes differently!* "The former has only to follow the pattern proposed to him by the latter. This latter is the mechanician who invents the machine; the former is merely the workman who sets it in motion."

What is Liberty?

"... **And, in fact, what is the political work which we are endeavoring to promote? It is no other than the instinctive effort of every people towards liberty**. And **what is liberty**, whose name can make every heartbeat, and which can agitate the world, **but the union of all liberties**, the liberty of conscience, of instruction, of association, of the press, of locomotion, of labour, and of exchange; in other words, the free exercise, for all, of all the inoffensive faculties; and again, in other words, the destruction of all despotisms, even of legal despotism, and **the reduction of law to its only rational sphere, which is to regulate the individual right of legitimate defense, or to repress injustice?"**

In order for liberty to exist, Governments must be restrained to that for which they were created – repressing injustice, and little else.

Are Politicians Greater Than Us?

"This tendency of the human race, it must be admitted, is greatly thwarted, particularly in our country, by the fatal disposition, resulting from classical teaching, and **common to all politicians, of placing themselves beyond mankind, to arrange, organize, and regulate it, according to their fancy."**

"...In general, however, these gentlemen, the reformers, legislators, and politicians, do not desire to exercise an immediate despotism over mankind. No, they are too moderate and too philanthropic for that. **They only contend for the despotism, the absolutism, the omnipotence of the law. They aspire only to make the law."** *And through the law, as Bastiat demonstrates, they work to accomplish their will, not necessarily the will of those they were elected to represent.*

"...One of the strangest phenomena of our time, and one which will probably be a matter of astonishment to our descendants, is **the doctrine which is founded upon**

this triple hypothesis: the radical passiveness of mankind, --the omnipotence of the law, --the infallibility of the legislator: this is the sacred symbol of the party which proclaims itself exclusively democratic. It is true that it professes also to be social. So far as it is democratic, it has an unlimited faith in mankind. So far as it is social, it places it beneath the mud." *And here we are many generations later, seeing much of the same thing!*

"...**But when once the legislator is duly elected,** then indeed the style of his speech alters. The nation is sent back into passiveness, inertness, nothingness, and **the legislator takes possession of omnipotence. It is for him to invent, for him to direct, for him to impel, for him to organize. Mankind has nothing to do but to submit;** the hour of despotism has struck.

And we must observe that this is decisive; for the people, just before so enlightened, so moral, so perfect, have no inclinations at all, or, if they have any, they all lead them downwards towards degradation." *Isn't this what we see in the United States now?*

"And yet they ought to have a little liberty!" *claim the politicians. But when we push for our liberty and ask* "What sort of liberty should be allowed to men?" *we are treated to their concerns:*

"**Liberty of conscience?** But we should see them all profiting by the permission to become atheists.

Liberty of education? But parents would be paying professors to teach their sons immorality and error; besides, if we are to believe M. Thiers, education, if left to the national liberty, would cease to be national, and we should be educating our children in the ideas of the Turks or Hindus, instead of which, thanks to the legal despotism of the universities, they have the good fortune to be educated in the noble ideas of the Romans.

Liberty of labour? But this is only competition, whose effect is to leave all productions unconsumed, to exterminate the people, and to ruin the tradesmen.

The liberty of exchange? But it is well known that the protectionists have shown, over and over again, that a man must be ruined when he exchanges freely, and that to become rich it is necessary to exchange without liberty.

Liberty of association? But, according to the socialist doctrine, liberty and association exclude each other, for the liberty of men is attacked just to force them to associate. **You must see, then, that**

the socialist democrats cannot in conscience allow men any liberty, because, by their own nature, they tend in every instance to all kinds of degradation and demoralization." *And what a price we pay for giving up our liberties!*

Bastiat goes on to ask the question we should ask of our legislators: "...The pretensions of organizers suggest another question, which I have often asked them, and to which I am not aware that I ever received an answer: **Since the natural tendencies of mankind are so bad that it is not safe to allow them liberty, how comes it to pass that the tendencies of organizers are always good?**

Do not the legislators and their agents form a part of the human race? Do they consider that they are composed of different materials from the rest of mankind? They say that society, when left to itself, rushes to inevitable destruction, because its instincts are perverse. **They pretend, to stop it in its downward course, and to give it a better direction.** They have, therefore, received from heaven, intelligence and virtues which place them beyond and above mankind: let them show their title to this superiority. **They would be our shepherds, and we are to be their flock. This arrangement presupposes in them a natural superiority, the right to which we are fully justified in calling upon them to prove."** *Have they proved their natural superiority to you? They have not proven it to me.*

"You must observe that I am not contending against their right to invent social combinations, to propagate them, to recommend them, and **to try them upon themselves, at their own expense and risk; but I**

do dispute their right to impose them upon us through the medium of the law, that is, by force and by public taxes.... To presume to have recourse to power and taxation, besides being oppressive and unjust, implies further, the injurious supposition that the organizer is infallible, and mankind incompetent."

Law is Justice

"What is law? What ought it to be? What is its domain? What are its limits? Where, in fact, does the prerogative of the legislator stop? I have no hesitation in answering, **Law is common force organized to prevent injustice; in short, Law is Justice**.

It is not true that the legislator has absolute power over our persons and property, since they pre-exist, and his work is only to secure them from injury. **It is not true that the mission of the law is to regulate our consciences, our ideas, our will, our education, our sentiments, our works, our exchanges, our gifts, our enjoyments.** Its mission is to prevent the rights of one from interfering with those of another, in any one of these things.

Law, because it has force for its necessary sanction, can only have as its lawful domain the domain of force, which is justice. And as every individual has a right to have recourse to force only in cases of lawful defense, so collective force, which is only the union of individual forces, cannot be rationally used for any other end.

The law, then, is solely the organization of individual rights, which existed before legitimate defense. Law is justice. So far from being able to oppress the persons of the people, or to plunder their property, even for a philanthropic end, its mission is to protect the former, and to secure to them the possession of the latter. It must not be said, either, that it may be philanthropic, so long as it abstains from all oppression; for this is a contradiction.

The law cannot avoid acting upon our persons and property; if it does not secure them, it violates them if it touches them. The law is justice." *How many fewer laws and regulations would exist if this simple understanding of law was followed?*

"Depart from this point, make the law religious, fraternal, equalizing, industrial, literary, or artistic, and you will be lost in vagueness and uncertainty; you will be upon unknown ground, in a forced Utopia, or, which is worse, in the midst of a multitude of Utopias, striving to gain possession of the law, and to impose it upon you; for fraternity and philanthropy have no fixed limits, like justice. **Where will you stop? Where is the law to stop?"** *And that is where we are today – where does it stop?*

"Does it follow that, if we are free, we shall cease to act? Does it follow, that if we do not receive an impulse from the law, we shall receive no impulse at all? Does it follow, that if the law confines itself to securing to us the free exercise of our faculties, our faculties will be paralyzed? Does it follow, that if the law does not impose upon us forms of religion, modes of association, methods of instruction, rules for labour, directions for exchange, and plans for charity, we shall plunge eagerly into atheism, isolation, ignorance, misery, and egotism? Does it follow, that we shall no longer recognize the power and goodness of God; that we shall cease to associate together, to help each other, to love and assist our unfortunate brethren, to study the secrets of nature, and to aspire after perfection in our existence?" *And, of course, Bastiat is telling us, we do not need law to make us practice our religion, our association, our charity, our education, etc. We need freedom from the law to do those things as we see fit.*

"Law is justice. And it is under the law of justice, under the reign of right, under the influence of liberty, security, stability, and responsibility, that every man will attain to the measure of his worth, to all the dignity of his being, and that mankind will accomplish, with order and with calmness--slowly, it is true, but with certainty--the progress decreed to it."

We can accomplish great things,

when Government gives us the liberty to do the things we need and want to do.

The Solution is Liberty

"...at whatever point of the scientific horizon I start from, I invariably come to the same thing - the solution of the social problem is in liberty. And have I not experience on my side? Cast your eye over the globe. **Which are the happiest, the most moral, and the most peaceable nations? Those where the law interferes the least with private activity; where the Government is the least felt; where individuality has the most scope, and public opinion the most influence;** where the machinery of the administration is the least important and the least complicated;

where taxation is lightest and least unequal, popular discontent the least excited and the least justifiable; **where the responsibility of individuals and classes is the most active,** and where, consequently, if morals are not in a perfect state, at any rate they tend incessantly to correct themselves; where transactions, meetings, and associations are the least fettered; where labour, capital, and production suffer the least from artificial displacements; where mankind follows most completely its own natural course; where the thought of God prevails the most over the inventions of men; those, in short, who realize the most nearly this idea-- That within the limits of right, all should flow from the free, perfectible, and voluntary action of man; nothing be attempted by the law or by force, except the administration of universal justice."

And it should be our goal, in our great country, to return as soon as possible to as close as we can to this state!

Conclusion

I hope you have enjoyed this brief look at Bastiat's Essays on Political Economy. *It is amazing to me how much of what he said is timeless – crossing international boundaries as well as still ringing true through the centuries. If you would like to read his complete work you can find it in various places on the internet, including www.Gutenberg.org.*

About the Author

Catherine Jaime did her undergraduate work at the Sloan School of Management at the Massachusetts Institute of Technology. She has taken additional economics training through the Foundation for Teaching Economics and the Foundation for Economic Education.

Catherine has taught high school economics and government. She has authored several books dealing with government and economics. She firmly believes in the importance of the U.S. Constitution and the free market, and it shows in her writings.

www.ingramcontent.com/pod-product-compliance
Lightning Source LLC
Chambersburg PA
CBHW061515180526
45171CB00001B/190